East of the Sandy

3rd in a Series

The

Columbia River

Highway

by Clarence E. Mershon

Books by Clarence E. Mershon

East of the Sandy Series:

Living East of the Sandy, Volume 1, ©1999
East of the Sandy, The Two World Wars, ©2001
East of the Sandy, The Columbia River Highway, ©2001

Soon to be published:

Living East of the Sandy, Volume 2

Others:

Corbett Now and Columbian Then, ©1999

East of the Sandy
The Columbia River Highway

This is the story of East Multnomah County farmers and loggers who helped build the Columbia River Highway (Columbia River Gorge section). It is also the story of their wives and children, who found employment in the restaurants, roadhouses, inns and other business establishments built to serve an ever-growing body of tourists that flocked to see the beautiful Columbia River Gorge; scenery that Samuel Lancaster's engineering marvel opened to all. The author documents the contributions of a remarkable group of political and business leaders whose vision, energy, hard work and philanthropy made the project possible. The highway, finally and belatedly recognized for its historic value by the State of Oregon, suffered severe damage to (or destruction of) many of its more remarkable features before it received the recognition and protection gained by its designation as the Historic Columbia River Highway.

Clarence E. Mershon

Grateful acknowledgment is given to the board and members of the Crown Point Country Historical Society, who encouraged my bringing this story to print. Special thanks to Rosetta (Henkle) Heitzman, who shared her father's written record of his participation in its construction; to Wesley Post, whose grandfather's photographs add much to the story; and to Steve Lehl, an avid collector of Gorge memorabilia. The planned program of the East Multnomah Pioneer Association for year-2002 will feature the history of the Columbia River Highway. This book is intended to add to Association's historical record concerning that era. Many thanks to those individuals in our community who have contributed their memories and pictures for the book. Again, the author appreciates Joan (Ellis) Benner's willingness to do an initial edit, which helped immensely. Also, many thanks to Sharon Nesbit, the *Gresham Outlook*, for her suggestions and comments. Finally, the author appreciates the suggestions, observations and information provided by Robert W. Hadlow, Senior Environmental Coordinator, Oregon Department of Transportation.

First Edition: Published in 2001.

International Standard Book Number
0-9717143-0-4

Published by Guardian Peaks, Inc., Portland, Oregon
Clarence Mershon
1220 N.E. 196th Avenue
Portland, Oregon 97230

Foreword

While Sam Hill is often mentioned as "the father of the Columbia River Highway," another individual, because of his efforts in getting the project underway, deserves accolades as well. Simon Benson, who made a fortune in Northwest forests, not only promoted the highway, but made significant contributions of time and money to expedite the work, both before and after construction began. His vision and philanthropy preserved significant and priceless areas for public access and use.

Simon Bergerson, born in Norway October 7, 1852, came with his family to the United States at age 16. An older brother, John, had emigrated five years earlier, taken a job in the Wisconsin woods and saved sufficient funds to pay for his family's passage to America on a sailing vessel. Once settled in Wisconsin, the family simplified its surname, changing it to Benson. In order to repay his brother for his passage, Simon took a job as a farm laborer. Once that obligation was paid, he married Esther Seale and opened a store in Lynxville, Wisconsin. In 1879, though the store had prospered, it burned with Benson's entire stock of merchandise. The loss was not covered by insurance, which necessitated his starting anew. Undaunted, Benson decided to move to Oregon, where he obtained work at a logging camp in Northwest Oregon.

In 1880, Benson purchased 160 acres of timber. The quarter-section contained several million feet of timber, causing Benson to decide to go into the timber business for himself. He purchased and trained a yoke of oxen, and was soon selling logs to the Northern Pacific Lumber Company. Within three years, he owned his land, equipment and stock free and clear. In 1883, however, his wife became ill, and Benson sold his holdings for six-thousand dollars and moved to Colfax, Washington, seeking a drier climate. Despite the move, his wife's health continued to deteriorate, and in 1890, she passed away, leaving Benson a widower with three children, Amos, Alice and Caroline. Upon Esther Benson's death, Benson decided to return to St. Helens, Oregon, where he re-entered the timber business.

Simon Benson soon entered into a partnership with Ordway and Weidler, to whom he had been selling logs. The partners purchased a large tract of timber, and built a logging railroad to transport logs from the woods. When the price of logs declined, both of Benson's partners decided to leave the business and sold their interests to Benson. Benson, always an innovator, experimented with using a donkey engine to yard logs, which practice he soon perfected. He also experimented with using log rafts to transport logs to California mills, again successfully, which saved him thousands of dollars per raft in shipping costs.

Eventually, Benson sold his timber holdings, sawmills and logging equipment for several million dollars, some of which he used to invest in other endeavors such as the Benson Hotel in Portland. He became interested in the 'good roads' movement, and his first public work involved that cause. He became the first Chairman of the newly formed Oregon Highway Commission. Numerous examples of his philanthropy directed toward the completion of the Columbia River Highway are documented in the text. Other acts are worthy of mention. When Hood River County issued seventy-five thousand dollars in highway bonds that went unsubscribed, Benson purchased the entire issue. Knowing the ill effects of the misuse of alcohol, Benson donated twenty bronze drinking fountains to the City of Portland so that loggers and other citizens would have easy access at several locations within the city to Portland's famous pure water.

With his record of business acumen, his leadership in business and civic affairs and his record of philanthropy, Benson earned and deserves an honored place in the hearts of Oregonians for his many contributions to the State. His legacy is recognized in the Gorge by such namesakes as Benson State Park and the Benson Footbridge at Multnomah Falls. (While tempted to include the Benson Plateau above Cascade Locks, that geographical feature was named for Thomas C. Benson, former local landowner with business interests in the Union Stockyards, Portland.) All who enjoy the Columbia River Gorge and the unsurpassed Historic Columbia River Highway are indebted to leaders such as Simon Benson.

Dedication

This book is dedicated to two early settlers: William F. Henkle and Charles W. Post. Henkle's daily record of his work on the Columbia River Highway, which his daughter, Rosetta (Henkle) Heitzman kindly allowed me to use, provided information regarding his (and others) participation in the construction project. Henkle settled on the 'hill' in 1907, leasing the Haynes Farm on Haynes (now Ogden) Road. In 1910, he purchased a farm in Springdale to which he moved his family in December, 1911. Examples of his daily notes are found starting on page six of the text. (My father, George 'Jum' Mershon, also worked on the highway, and related some of his experiences on the job, including the story of the collapse of the Nielson Bridge [p. 20]).

Charles W. Post, born in Galion, Ohio, February 22, 1858, came to Oregon in 1907. At the age of sixteen he traveled to Europe, determined to study works of the European Masters. Accepted at the Ecole des Beaux Arts in Paris, he studied under Piloty and the sculptor Guillaume. He spent two years in Florence, Italy, where he studied under William T. Dannat. Finally, in quest of learning more about his true love, etching, Post applied for admittance at the Royal Academy in Munich, where he studied under the master engraver, William Unger. Post returned to the United States in the fall of 1878, enthralled by the works of the masters he had seen, most particularly by those of Rembrandt, considered the absolute master of the engraving art.

Post established a studio on an acre of land at Chanticleer Point in 1912. Later the Richfield Oil Company placed a large advertising sign on the site, which soon blew away when the areas well-known east wind came up. The Company replaced the sign, but made certain the second effort could withstand hurricane force winds. The concrete piers for this sign remain on the site, though the sign they supported is long gone.

Post sold his art works at his studio. His paintings hang in many homes in the community. A Post portrait of my mother, holding her first child, hung in our home for years. Fortunately, Post carried a camera with him as he searched for subjects in the environs of the Gorge. Consequently, he left a legacy of photographs that capture the era when the highway was built. Post's grandson, Wesley Post, kindly permitted the author to use this material. This, together with Henkle's written record, provided the stimulus for the author to write of this momentus event and how it affected the lives of Gorge residents.

Post planned to publish a complete series of etchings of the Columbia River Gorge, similar to his earlier work published in St. Paul, Minnesota. He installed an etching press in 1921 with the hope that this long-held objective would be fulfilled. Unfortunately, in the spring of 1922, after a short illness, Charles W. Post passed away, age 64.

Will F. Henkle, Farmer

Charles W. Post, Artist

The Columbia River Highway
Contents

The View West From Crown Point c1915

Rooster Rock (right foreground), McGowan's salmon cannery (center), John Sweeney's farm (left), tunnel point (left center-leveled and now a parking pull-off on I-84), and the Columbia River. Note the train approaching Rooster Rock Station and the riverboat in the channel.

Photo courtesy of Wes Post.

Early 'Roads' Through the Gorge

According to pioneer lore, an Indian trail came through the Gorge on the south side of the Columbia River. This trail connected two important Indian trading sites: Celilo Falls east of The Dalles, and the Oregon City Falls on the Willamette (Multnomah) River. When a telegraph line was strung through the Gorge to connect Portland with points east, the line followed this ancient trail, and thus, the trail became known as the 'wire trail.' Crossing the Sandy River in the vicinity of Troutdale, the wire trail followed the east bank of the river to a point about 150 yards east of the bridge, where it left the river bank to ascend the bluff to the relatively flat bench above. According to anecdotal reports of highway worker families, when the bridge across the Sandy at Troutdale was built in 1912-13, many Indian artifacts were found at the east end of the bridge. According to oral histories, Indians told early settlers that a village beside the Sandy River at this point had been covered by a rock slide. Glenora Emily, in her journal, mentioned that she was told this tale "by Old Indian John, a little old dried up fellow some said to be 120 years old. I knew him when I was first married to Jack Vandever and lived near Fairview. He stopped many times and I'd give him doughnuts and a cup of coffee. He'd pour it in his saucer and drink it by putting his face down and supping it up. He said he might spill it on my white tablecloth, his hands shook so."

Glenora reported that Charlie Bramhall, a County roadboss during the highway's construction, brought some of these artifacts to his home, including one that sat on his front porch for many years. She wrote, "...Someone gave his wife, Alma (Bramhall), a carved rock 'turtle' grinding bowl found there (at the Troutdale bridge)." The object to which Glenora refers (see p. 2) remains in the Bramhall family; it now belongs to Bramhall's granddaughter, Pat (Bramhall) Paget. Its existence lends credence to Indian John's tale.

Once on the flat, the trail continued across the present Seidl Road, angling in a southeast direction. It crossed Ogden Road below what is now Hurt Road and slightly above Mershon Road. From a point just east of the Klinski farm, Wand Road followed the path of the wire trail to the point where it makes a near 90 degree turn northward. At that corner, the wire trail continued almost directly east along the boundary between the Jasper Mershon and Sakajiro Takeuchi family properties. Native arti-

1

Native Artifact Found by Highway Workers

Workers uncovered this "turtle" grinding bowl at the north end of the Troutdale bridge while constructing the Columbia River Highway. It measures approximately 9" by 12". The 'turtle's head is to the right; its tail to the left. The bowl is now in the possession of Pat (Bramhall) Paget, Charlie Bramhall's granddaughter. *Photo by the author.*

facts have been found on the Mershon place at a spring below (south of) the trail. In this section, the trail followed the rim of the flat above Mershon Road where the sidehills slope to the south toward Springdale. Coming off the flat, the Dunn family driveway (where the Matsuba family lived prior to World War II) followed the former trail to a point close to the intersection of Mershon and Chamberlain Roads. The author hiked this old trail many, many times between this point and where it became part of Wand Road, as it served as a shortcut to his Uncle Jasper Mershon's home and his Uncle Ray Wilson's home, both of which were then located on Wand Road.

From this point eastward, the trail is part of or ran nearly parallel to Mershon Road until it reached the present route of the Columbia River Highway about a mile west of Corbett. It crossed the former Kincaid place (now owned by the Bates family) and Mershon Road in the vicinity of the present location of the Corbett Christian Church. Thence, the Columbia River Highway followed the ancient pathway rather closely until it reached Chanticleer Point (now Portland Women's Forum State Scenic Overlook). According to Clara (Lasley) Salzman, a partially imbedded insulator in the old maple tree in front of the church at its former

Portions of the Old Wire Trail

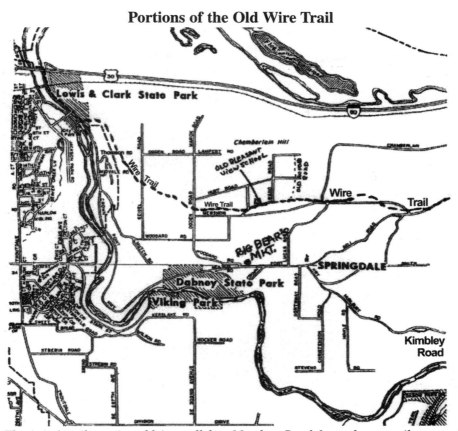

The 'wire' trail ran (roughly) parallel to Mershon Road from about a mile west of Corbett to Ogden Road, then ran northwestward to the Sandy River. In early days, settlers on the 'hill' used it to reach Troutdale.   *Map courtesy of Sharon Nesbit.*

location marked the trail through Corbett. At the Overlook, the highway and the wire trail part, as the wagon road from Chanticleer to Rooster Rock essentially followed the wire trail to the river bank below. (Chanticleer Point and Dalton Point, near Bridal Veil, have also been rich sources of native artifacts.) From Rooster Rock, the trail apparently continued eastward along the river bank to Latourell, Bridal Veil, Warrendale and beyond. From Latourell eastward, it is certain that the highway intercepted the trail at many points. In 1855, according to observations of Lieutenant Henry L. Abbot of the U.S. Corps of Engineers, two "pack trails" followed the south shore of the Columbia, one of which was "not passable during high water."

On January 24, 1856, legislation establishing a territorial road from the Sandy River (Troutdale) to The Dalles passed. Construction commenced on a wagon road between Bonneville (the lower Cascades) and

Cascade Locks (the upper Cascades) almost immediately. The following year, legislation passed authorizing the construction of a wagon road and bridge across Eagle Creek. In 1863, a trail for pack trains and cattle opened on the Oregon side to serve as a route to the mines in the interior. In 1872, the Oregon Legislature appropriated $50,000 for the construction of a wagon road from the Sandy River through to The Dalles. Four years later, an additional $50,000 was appropriated for the project. The resulting wagon road was 12-feet wide, but it was both crooked and steep. Partially obliterated by the construction of the Oregon Washington Railroad and Navigation Company line in 1883, this military (or county) road also suffered extensively from the high water and flooding of 1894. Traces of this road were found by crews when the survey of the Columbia River Highway was completed in Hood River County during the winter of 1913-14, and some masonry-walled sections are still visible above I-84 on Shellrock Moutain. (From "Tentative Dates Pertaining to Road Building in the Columbia Gorge, 1850-1960," by E. Walton, published in 1967.)

Before the highway was built, most East County residents used Baseline Road (Stark Street) to reach Troutdale, Gresham or Portland. From Portland, the traveler followed Baseline past Twelve-mile Road (and the Twelve-Mile Roadhouse) to reach Troutdale Road. Here, a choice was made; turn north to reach Troutdale, or turn south to continue east. The eastbound resident turned right at Troutdale Road, continuing for about one-half mile, then turned eastward once again on Sweetbriar Road. When Kerslake Road was reached, the traveler turned left toward the Sandy River, reaching the Portland Auto Club grounds (built in 1912) and the Nielson Bridge. Across the river, the road turned eastward toward Springdale. In Springdale, the road passed the post office (near the present Northway Road) and took a left at the Y near True's store and the schoolhouse (Bell Grade). The road to the right led to Gordon Creek, Aims and Bull Run. The road eastward continued through (Upper) Corbett, following the old wire trail to Chanticleer. At Upper Corbett, a branch road to the right led to Hurlburt and Gordon Creek; a branch road to the left led to Corbett (now Lower Corbett, or Corbett Station.) At Chanticleer Point, a road followed the former wire trail to Rooster Rock Landing and the railway station. Beyond Chanticleer, the traveler continued about one-half mile to Brower Road (now Larch Mountain Road), following it for about a mile before turning left on the road to Latourell.

The Twelve-Mile Roadhouse

The building housing the Twelve-Mile Roadhouse, located on the south side of Baseline Road (Stark Street) near the 12-mile post, was moved from the site of the Lewis and Clark Exposition in 1906. It burned in 1939.   *Photo courtesy of Rosetta Henkle.*

Just before Latourell was reached, a branch road to the right led to Bridal Veil and also to Brower.

A couple of abortive attempts to complete a road through the Gorge came in 1910, when Multnomah County started the construction of a road from Bridal Veil to the Hood River County line. A dispute with the Oregon Railroad and Navigation Company concerning the right-of-way stopped the effort. In 1912, Governor Oswald West provided prison labor to Hood River County to construct a road around the base of Shellrock Mountain, but the effort failed because of difficulties presented by its talus slopes. Simon Benson donated $10,000 to help fund this experiment. However, the effort stimulated interest in building a highway through the Gorge, as envisioned by Sam Hill. In February, 1913, Hill invited potential backers of the highway (including the entire Oregon legislature) to his Maryhill Estate to view the Estate's newly built, paved-road system constructed under the supervision of Samuel Lancaster. Later that year, Multnomah County Commissioners hired Lancaster as Consulting Engineer on Hill's recommendation. On November 25, 1913, County Roadmaster John B. Yeon proposed extending Baseline Road (Stark Street) from Troutdale Road to the "automobile club's resort" on the Sandy River.

Construction Phase

On December 16, 1913, William F. 'Will' Henkle's laconic entries upon his *Fireman's Fund Insurance Company* calendar changed. Abruptly, the routine, more customary 'farm' entries were displaced. Entries such as these: Monday, December 8, 1913, *"Dug spuds most all day;"* Friday, December 12, *"Dug carrots all day, terrible east wind;"* and Saturday, December 13, *"Worked in woodshed, got pig from Emily,"* were replaced. The first example: Tuesday, **December 16, 1913**, *"Worked on road at bridge near Troutdale."* On both December 19 and 20, the "on road" entry appears and continues week days through December 30. The entries resume Thursday, January 15, 1914: *"Work on road with team 1/2 (day), with shovel 1/2 (day),"* and a similar entry is found January 16. 'Road' entries continue from Monday, February 16, 1914, through the month, when more typical 'farm' entries resume. For a period of about two years, such 'road' entries are interspersed with his more typical 'farm' entries.

During the summer, for example, the following 'farm' entries are found: July 3, 1914, *"Finish haying at home. Wand came;"* July 4, *"Go to Troutdale celebration, ice cream .25, pop .35, firecrackers .25, cigars .25";...July 17, "Shocked hay for G (Gib Bates):"* July 18, ... *"took sow to Roy Emilys;"*...August 1, *"Ed Woodard cut 5 acres grain, 3 balls twine;"* August 2, *"Finish shocking grain...go to Bram for berries."* However, on August 5, 1914, the "On road" entries resume, but with a slight modification. For example the notation August 5 states: *"On road, $2.25."* On September 25, he wrote: *"On road 1/2 day. Ready to use team on road."* The notation the following day reads: *"On road with team."* No 'road' entries appear until Monday, February 8, 1915, when this entry appears: *"Work on road with team $5.00."* Similar entries continue somewhat regularly thereafter until Monday, May 31. The entry that day reads: *"Last day on road."* The entry August 26, 1915 states: *"Finished (roofing the Grange) Hall and drove over highway."* On Saturday, August 28, 1915, the "On road with team" entries resume, concluding with this final entry on Monday, October 25, 1915: *"On road 2 hrs. for County, 7½ hours for Warren Company."* On December 27, 1915, Henkle wrote: *"Snowed some - go to see highway with Bramhall."* These calendar 'road' entries document Will Henkle's unsuspecting participation in one of the

Columbia River Highway Work Crew c1914

Eugene Berney holds the team on the left; George 'Jum' Mershon and Louis Nelson kneel on the right in front of the other team. Others in the picture are not known.
Photo, the author.

great engineering accomplishments of the century, the construction of the Columbia River Highway.

Elizabeth Salt, in her book, *Mighty Engineering Feats*, ranked the highway among such other engineering marvels as the first continental railroad, the New York City water supply system, the Panama Canal, Boulder Dam and the Golden Gate and San Francisco Bay Bridges. Also, the timing of the entries reflect what was happening with certain phases of the road construction. Henkle was one of a large number of local farmers who worked on what became the Columbia River Highway (now the Historic Columbia River Highway). The work undoubtedly gave each of them an opportunity to earn money to supplement the sometimes uncertain income from the farm.

Henkle's final 'road' entry, indicating that he worked for the "Warren Company" in October, 25, 1915, is significant. In an election held April 14, 1915, Multnomah County voters approved a bond issue for $1,250,000 to pave the highway from Portland to the Hood River County line. Amos S. Benson and John B. Yeon spearheaded the spring campaign, which resulted in overwhelming support for the job. The contract, awarded June 17, 1915, called for the highway to be paved with

Springdale and Corbett Area Farmers Work on the Highway

Standing, L to R: Frank Fehrenbacher, unknown, Walt Preston, unknown, unknown and Christen 'Cook' Christensen. Seated, unknown, unknown, George Nelson, George 'Jum' Mershon and unknown.   *Photo, the author.*

"Warrenite" for most of its near sixty-mile length. Warrenite was an aggregate of gravel and larger rocks (2 - 5 inches) bonded together into a relatively smooth surface. The specifications provided for an eighteen foot surface with a two-foot shoulder on each side (the minimum width for the highway was 24 feet, except for the viaducts, which were 20 feet). Paving was completed in October, hence Henkle's final work day may have coincided with the completion of the contract. After the highway was paved, motorists could drive the Multnomah County segment of the highway, see the waterfalls and reach Bonneville on a smooth, hard-surfaced highway.

Dedication ceremonies for the official opening of the Columbia River Highway were held on June 7, 1916, at three locations: Crown Point, Benson Park and Multnomah Falls. The ceremony dedicating the eastern portion occurred on July 7, 1916. Completion of the work brought national and international attention and honors to Samuel C. Lancaster, Consulting Engineer in charge of its design and execution. A plaque at Crown Point honors Lancaster with these words:

"Samuel C. Lancaster, 1864-1941. Chief Engineer, Scenic Columbia River Highway 1913-1915. Pioneer Builder of Hard-Sur-

8

'Crown Point' Before the Highway

Thor's Point stood above the seining grounds below and provided inhabitants with an inspiring view of the Columbia River Gorge. Charles Post took this picture of his pet goat standing on the Point. After Samuel Lancaster gave it a 'crown,' the landmark became known as Crown Point. Two landowners, Lorens M. Lund and Osman Royal, donated land at the point to Multnomah County.   *Photo courtesy of Wes Post.*

face Roads. His Genius Overcame Tremendous Obstacles, Extending and Replacing The Early Trail Through The Columbia River Gorge With A Highway of Poetry And Drama So That Millions Could Enjoy God's Spectacular Creations."

In making his original survey, starting in the fall of 1913, Lancaster, described as a "brilliant engineer with the soul of a poet," clambered through the forest, beneath the palisades, along the precipices and around the natural buttresses of the Gorge. He found himself surrounded by unsurpassed beauty. After the highway was completed, he remarked: "My love for the beautiful is inherited from my mother. When I made my preliminary survey here and found myself standing waste-deep in ferns, I remembered my mother's long ago warning, 'Oh Samuel, do be careful of my Boston Fern.' And I then pledged myself that none of the wild beauty should be marred where it could be prevented. The highway was so built that not one tree was felled, not one fern crushed, unnecessarily."

Certainly, part of Lancaster's inspiration to build such a magnificent highway resulted from a visit to Europe in 1908 with Samuel Hill, Major Henry L. Bowlby and Reginald H. Thomson, Seattle Parks Department Commissioner. Both Bowlby and Lancaster were on the staff at

9

The Gorge As Lancaster Found It c 1913

The Gorge from Crown Point, with 'Big Island' (pioneer name) in the left foreground, Latourell, mid-picture on the right, and Bridal Veil in the distance. The home built by John T. Smith in 1900 can be seen on the Island.   Photo courtesy of Wes Post.

the University of Washington, participants in its new highway engineering program. Lancaster had completed Lake Washington Boulevard in Seattle for Thomson the previous year. Hill, past-president of the American Roadbuilders Association and a visionary with a passion for good roads, took Lancaster, Thomson and Bowlby to the First International Road Congress in Paris, to which Hill was a delegate. The group took the opportunity to view some of the outstanding highways on the continent. Their tour took them along the Rhine River, where, between Koblenz and Wiesbaden, they viewed the Ruedesheim Burg. This castle overlooks terraced vineyards supported by dry masonry walls built on the steep slopes above the Rhine. These stone walls, built during the era of Charlemagne, became the inspiration for the rock walls of the Columbia River Highway. In Italy the group found Italian workmen who continued to practice the rock-laying skills of that earlier era. A visit to Switzerland took them to the famed Axenstrasse and its three-windowed tunnel carved through solid rock that provided an outstanding view of Switzerland's Lake Lucerne and the mountains surrounding the lake. Certainly, this model provided the inspiration for the five-windowed tunnel at Mitchell Point. In the foreword of his book, *The Columbia, America's Great Highway*, Lancaster pays tribute to Sam Hill:

10

Memorial to Sam Hill, Road Builder

This monument, erected to honor Sam Hill, is located at the Portland Women's Forum Park at Chanticleer Point, where the former road to Rooster Rock landing intersects the Columbia River Highway. The large boulder came from Rocky Butte in S.E. Portland. It was placed at the site in 1932.   Photo courtesy of Steve Lehl.

Samuel Hill, Roadbuilder

"Who loves this country and brought me to it. Who showed me the German Rhine and Continental Europe. Whose kindness made it possible for me to have a part in planning and constructing this great highway.

There is a time and place for every man to act his part in life's drama and to build according to his ideals.

God shaped these great mountains round about us, and lifted up those mighty domes into a region of perpetual snow.

He fashioned the Gorge of the Columbia, fixed the course of the broad river, and caused the crystal streams both small and great, to leap down from the crags and sing their never ending songs of joy.

Then He planted a garden, men came and built a beautiful city close by the wonderland. To some He gave great wealth - to every man his talent, - and when the time had come for men to break down the mountain barriers, construct a great highway of

11

A Waterfall on Oneonta Creek

Lancaster: "(God) caused crystal streams, both small and great, to leap down from the crags and sing their never ending songs of joy." Photo courtesy of Wes Post.

commerce, and utilize the beautiful, which is "as useful as the useful;" He set them to the task and gave to each his place.

I am thankful to God for His goodness in permitting me to have a part in building this broad thoroughfare as a frame to the beautiful picture which He created."
Samuel Christopher Lancaster, 1915

Sam Hill is often referred to as "the father of the Columbia River Highway." Certainly his ideas and vision influenced both Bowlby and Lancaster. When the Oregon State Highway Commission was established in 1913, Major Bowlby became the first State Highway Engineer, and Lancaster, his assistant. In the "Preface" to his book, Lancaster states:

"While engaged as Consulting Engineer in fixing the location and directing the construction of the Columbia River Highway from Portland east through the Cascade Range in Multnomah County, Oregon, I studied the landscape with much care and became acquainted with its formation and its geology. I was profoundly impressed by its majestic beauty and marveled at the creative power of God, who made it all.

The everchanging lights and shadows from morning until night, made pictures rare and beautiful, which always charmed me... As I climbed about the steep slopes of the mountains, where in places it was necessary to use ropes for safety, I thought of the many hardships endured by the early explorers when they came into the Oregon country.

'Road Boss' Charlie Bramhall

Charlie Bramhall at home with his wife, Alma.   Photo courtesy of Pat Paget.

To every man who had a part in the construction of the Columbia River Highway through the Cascade Mountains to the sea; from the humblest laborer, to the Governor of the great State of Oregon, I say with all my heart, 'I thank you for the help you gave; we could not have succeeded without you.'"

The "humblest laborers" included many East Multnomah County farmers. Among those who worked on the highway, many for roadboss Charlie Bramhall, were: Roy Anderson, Harley Bates, Eugene 'Gene' Berney, Christen 'Cook' Christensen, Frank Fehrenbacher, Albert Graff, William 'Will' Henkle, Willis Hicks, Frank Knieriem, George Knieriem, Robert 'Bob' Larson, Walter Mannthey, George 'Jum' Mershon, Roy Muck, George Nelson, Louis Nelson, Walt Preston, Nelson Ross, William Ross, Albert Salzman and Jacob Seidl. In addition to Will Henkle, others using a team included David Benfield, Sam Hulit (team and wagon), Art Ledbury (team and Fresno [horse-drawn scraper]), Charlie Lofstedt (team and skid), Ben Luscher (team pulling a Fresno), Fritz Luscher (team and Fresno), Alfred D. Mershon (team and wagon), Louis 'Bill' Mershon (team and wagon), Fred Shoultz (team and wagon), and James C. Wilson (team pulling a Fresno). Shoultz hauled rock from lower Corbett that was used by Italian laborers in building the highway's celebrated rock walls. Art Johnson served on the crew that slashed brush and cleared the right-of-way. Later he also provided a team that pulled a Fresno. In 1915, laborers received $2.50 per 10-hour day and a man with a team, $5.00 per day.

In keeping with the times, women served in a supporting role. Bessie Knieriem prepared and took lunches to her brothers working on the road, which is how she met her future husband, Roy Muck. Della Henkle prepared breakfasts for the road crew during the time they worked in the vicinity. She also put up box lunches for them, which permitted her to earn some extra household money. Rosetta Henkle, 5 years of age at the time, remembered that road workers called her "Merry Sunshine." Charlie and Alma Bramhall boarded highway workers, who dearly loved Alma's celebrated bread rolls. In March, 1914, Multnomah County built a camp near the 'summit' to accommodate 135 highway workers. Joe Dobing cooked meals for the men during the time the camp was used. The men paid twenty-five cents per meal. A Mr. Speaker was in charge of the camp. According to the *Gresham Outlook* ("Columbia Heights," May 26, 1914), Roy Anderson and William Ross had the "honor of moving the first scraper of dirt" for the 'Heights' section of the new highway. According to pioneer records, Alex Barr worked on the highway, serving as road supervisor and camp foreman (see "Francis P. Hickey," *Pioneer History*, p.99).

Lancaster, in his book, honors John B. Yeon: "A wealthy and public-spirited citizen of Portland, (Yeon) volunteered to give, without remuneration, his entire time to this splendid work...Mr. Yeon's long experience in handling men in lumber camps fitted him admirably for this great task. His sagacity and love of the beautiful enabled him to grasp the meaning of the Engineer's plans, and thus to decide important matters correctly and with great dispatch." Yeon directed the actual construction of the highway as Multnomah County Roadmaster. From 1913-1917, Yeon worked on the project for a dollar per year. On August 11, 1915, Julius Meier, President of the Columbia Highway Association, presented Mr. Yeon with a beautiful gold-lined silver loving cup, which bore this inscription:

To
John B. Yeon
Roadmaster, Citizen, Husband, Father, Friend

Who, seeking to serve others found a new happiness for himself. May others drink from this never failing cup and find the draft as sweet.   Portland, Ore., August 11, 1915.

The names of the donors were engraved on the reverse side. These included the names of the prominent citizens of Portland who had initiated, supported and helped bring to fruition the construction of the Columbia River Highway:

Amos S. Benson	**Simon Benson**	**H.L. Bowlby**
Samuel Hill	**Rufus C. Holman**	**C.S. Jackson**
Samuel Lancaster	**Julius H. Meier**	**Frank Terrace**
Oswald West	**John F. Carroll**	**H.L. Pittock**

The Eastern Approach to Multnomah Falls c1915

This photograph, looking west toward Multnomah Falls, shows the highway before it was paved. Fortunately for travelers, portions of the highway were paved in 1915. Visible to the right of the tracks is a steamboat at the Multnomah Falls Landing. The point beyond the landing is the present location of the parking lot on I-84 at Multnomah Falls. The convenience of highway travel soon caused the demise of the riverboats. *Photo courtesy of Wes Post.*

Paving the Highway

Despite continuous opposition from some taxpayers, a portion of the highway was paved in 1915. At a meeting held in November, 1913, John B. Yeon introduced a plan to extend Baseline Road (Stark Street) to the Sandy River, and spend $900,000 on road improvements. The discussions continued through 1914. The *Gresham Outlook*, March 27, 1914, reported "Hard Surface Discord," and on March 31, 1914, that "Commissioners plan to go ahead with plans to hard surface Baseline." In late November, 1914, County Commissioners proposed paving the section from the Troutdale bridge to the highway, and paving the Columbia River Highway to the County line. The controversy continued, but good sense finally prevailed as voters approved the bond issue, as mentioned earlier. The Warren Company gained the contract awarded in June, 1915, for paving the Multnomah County section of the highway to the Hood River County line. The Company completed the approximate 60-mile paving job by late October that year.

15

"Hot Stuff" - Paving Material for the Highway

Sam Hulit, with his team and wagon, heads for the Corbett 'batch plant' for another load. This view of the highway is at Corbett, approaching the plant from the east. Hulit is on the highway west of the future site of George Chamberlain's store.

Photo by Laura Mershon.

The paving material, "Warrenite," a conglomerate of rock and gravel bonded with bitumen, was labeled "hot stuff" by workers on the job. The Warren Company called it "bitulithic pavement." The paving material was mixed and heated at "batch plants" set-up at various locations to provide the paving material. One "batch plant" was located in Corbett, directly across from the old Columbian High School. Local farmers, with teams and wagons, hauled the material to the job site. In somewhat of a departure from the labor-intensive methods used to grade the highway, a mechanical roller was used to pack the paving material. A crusher placed on the Ross farm near Chanticleer Point provided gravel for the highway. Chester 'Chet' Knieriem gained experience working there that led to a career in the road construction field. (After the job on the highway was completed, Warren Construction Company sent him to Victoria, B.C. to manage its crusher there.) Another source of rock for the highway was the Reed Quarry near Tunnel #1. Of course, additional contracts were awarded after the initial one granted to the Warren Company. At an observance held near Rowena June 27, 1922, Simon Benson, honored for his role in bringing the highway into existence, ceremoniously spread the last bit of paving mixture that completed the paving of the highway from Astoria to The Dalles.

After the highway was paved, East County residents continued to be involved working on the highway. Two local farmers, Frank Knieriem

The Corbett "Batch Plant," c1915

The "batch plant" at Corbett was located across from the original Columbian High School, which is seen in the background across the highway from the plant. This building burned July 3, 1922. The (fire-gutted) historic grade school building is now located on the site. Note the bell tower of the high school is not finished. It was completed by 1917.   *Photo by Laura Mershon.*

and Dave Butler, painted the yellow center stripe from the Summit to Latourell by hand. After a major snowstorm closed the road in 1921, a number of local farmers, including Ig Wand and Bob Knieriem, helped clear the highway of snowdrifts near Oneonta. A Springdale resident also worked on the highway for several years. Louise (Rackliff) Ports, a very talented artist, painted and lettered highway signs from Troutdale to the Hood River County line. According to reports, it was an ordinary sight, while motoring the Gorge highway, to see Louise Ports on a ladder painting a road sign. She carried a short ladder, paints and other materials in the trunk of her Ford coupe. Later, she obtained employment with the Robinson Neon Sign Company as a painter. Her son, Jay Ports, also took up the work and joined his mother working for the same firm.

From Troutdale, the highway continues westward through Parkrose and follows Sandy Boulevard into Portland. Crossing the Fremont Bridge, 'US 30' signs direct the traveler westward along the Columbia River to Astoria, the western terminus of the fabled highway. Much of the highway west of Portland was realigned and/or widened years ago.

The Original Tads

Tad's, formerly located on the east bank of the Sandy River at the north approach to the bridge at Troutdale, became a popular stop for both tourists and local patrons in the '30s. *Photo courtesy of the Troutdale Historical Society.*

A Tour Back in Time

The western terminus of the 'Gorge' segment of the highway is just west of Troutdale. From the Troutdale City Hall (which is 1.3 miles from the highway's western terminus) on Troutdale's main street (the Columbia River Highway), the visitor starts an interesting (oftentimes imaginary) journey back in time. After crossing the steel bridge (m 1.8) over the Sandy River, completed in 1912, the Columbia River Highway followed the old wire trail along the east bank of the Sandy a short distance to where the wire trail left the river and turned up the embankment, as mentioned earlier. The original Tad's Tap Pot Inn, built in the late '20s by Tad Johnson, was located at the northern end of the bridge (m 1.9 l). The connecting road from the Columbia River Highway to Lewis and Clark State Park and I-84 displaced the Inn in the late '40s. Tad's became a 'must' stop for farmers on their way to and from town. It was (and continues to be) a popular eating establishment, though it has changed owners (and location). Judy Jones now owns Tad's. The highway continues along the Sandy River past Tad's, the former Foothill Service Station (m 2.6 l) and the Tippie Canoe. Beyond the latter, the former Big Bend Tavern (m 4.1 r) comes into view. This establishment took its name from

Tad's Restaurant c2001

The relocated Tad's restaurant, now owned by Judy Jones, is situated on the east bank of the Sandy River about a half-mile from the Troutdale Bridge. It has been at this location for more than 50 years.   *Photo, the author.*

The Upper Bridge Across the Sandy River c1916

This photograph of the Stark Street Bridge, from the Portland Auto Club grounds on the left (south) approach across the river to the bluff, also shows the 'Troutdale to Stark Street Bridge' section of the Columbia River Highway under construction on the north bank of the Sandy River (completed in 1916). Photo postcard courtesy of Steve Lehl.

the 'Big Bend' in the Sandy, where the river makes a sweeping turn to the north. Formerly a restaurant and auto court, the Big Bend has long since closed.

19

Next, the Stark Street Bridge (m 4.4 r), built in 1914, can be seen. This bridge replaced the 30-year old Nielson Bridge, which collapsed on (Good Roads' Day) April 25, 1914, with a load of gravel intended for the new highway. The gravel had been loaded by a 5-man crew at the Baker Pit (on Stark Street past Troutdale Road, now part of the grounds of Mt. Hood Community College). Upon the return trip, the weight of the gravel and its five-man crew caused the bridge to give way, dumping the men into the river below. Fortunately, the most serious injury was a broken arm suffered by roadboss Charlie Bramhall. The driver, Christen 'Cook' Christensen, and laborers, Frank Fehrenbacher, George 'Jum' Mershon and Louis 'Bill' Mershon, came

Campbell's Flower Stand

Casner 'Shorty' Campbell (right) sold cut flowers at his road side stand near Springdale.
Photo courtesy of Belle Evans.

through essentially unscathed, except, as the *Gresham Outlook* reported, "for a cold dip in the river." At the south end of the Stark Street (upper) Bridge, the Portland Auto Club had earlier built a facility for its members, which came to be known as Viking Park. In 1921, S.G. Ruth rented the facility and opened The Bluebird Inn. The area is now a private residence owned by Junki and Linda Yoshida.

Continuing on the main highway, notice Dabney State Park on the right, where the highway starts its ascent along the bluff above the Sandy River. The Park, named for the former owner of the property, includes picnicking and other outdoor recreational opportunities. In former days, beyond Dabney and approaching a long, sweeping curve to the left, the Campbell family flower stand (m 5.3 l), featured gladiolas, daffodils and other locally grown blooms during the growing season. After negotiating the curve, the highway leaves the Sandy River as it approaches Springdale.

Springdale now (2001) hosts few businesses compared to the village existing when the highway was the principal arterial east. In the mid-'20s, Springdale (m 5.8) had four stores, a campground, a meat market,

The General Store in Springdale c1933

This store, established by William Northway in September 1912, continued in operation for more than thirty years. In 1933, the store was owned by Lloyd Bramhall. While the store is gone, a storage building formerly attached to the store at its east end has been converted to apartments, and still stands.

Photo courtesy of Pat (Bramhall) Paget.

three service stations, a hotel with a barber shop, two garages (one of which sold new automobiles), a shop for appliances and electrical supplies, a dance hall, a feed store, an ice cream shop, a cabinet shop, lockers, an Odd Fellows Lodge and the Springdale Grade School. Where Woodard Road intersects the highway, Ralph Sanders operated a filling station (likely built by Erick Enquist) that served travelers attracted by the new highway; the Springdale Fire Station is now situated on the site. The Big Bear Country Market and Deli is adjacent to the east, while Crown Point Automotive (l) and Mom's Garden Bakery and Cafe (Blue House-r) are located farther east. George and Louise Ports once operated a fruit stand where the automotive business is located. The Ports catered to local people as well as travelers; many sight-seeing buses stopped at the stand to allow passengers to buy farm fresh fruit and apple cider.

The vacant lot beyond Mom's (r) is where Jack Zilm and Hans Hendrickson built a dance hall, which William Northway converted to a general store in 1912. After the reconstruction, William Northway moved the merchandise from his first store on Northway Road to the building. In 1919, Northway sold the store to James C. 'Curly' Wilson, who also owned and operated two milk routes he had purchased earlier from Ben Bruger. The milk routes involved picking up milk from local dairy farmers and delivering it to a creamery in Portland. Since many farmers ordered groceries to be delivered by the milk truck, purchasing the general

Springdale Grade School c1938

Springdale Grade School, located on the north side of the highway near its intersection with Bell Grade, was built by Cecil Pounder in 1932. Founded in 1898, the District consolidated with the Corbett in 1960.   Photo courtesy of Rosetta Henkle.

store seemed to be a natural adjunct to the business. Wilson sold both the store and the milk routes to George Atkinson. In the '20s, George Atkinson built an addition at the east end of the store for storage. Subsequent owners included Lloyd Bramhall and William Mishey. After the store was razed, Ridge Law remodeled the storage building to provide cold storage lockers for local residents. Later the building was converted to apartments.

The adjacent lot immediately east of this building held Roy Parson's garage and Edna Parson's candy and ice cream shop. In 1922, Parson and Tom Northway added a garage to Van Zandt's blacksmith shop, which they had purchased earlier. To the east, just beyond Northway Road, a traveler found an autocamp with camping facilities. The two-story building that housed the former hotel and barber shop (m 6.1 r) stands adjacent to the Springdale Tavern. The tavern occupies a former market and part of the historic Salzman garage. Fred Salzman and Harley Bates built the garage in 1915 to serve auto traffic on the new highway. A confectionary and barber shop were added in 1922 and, in 1923, the Springdale Hotel. Mr. C.E. Vest managed both the hotel and the adjacent market when it opened. In the late '20s, Mr and Mrs. Sam Shaw managed the hotel and C. Thatcher, the barber shop. Next (left) is the former Springdale Grade School (built by Cecil Pounder Construction in 1932) and Ridge & Son Millwork (just beyond Bell Grade - the shop was built for Vern Lucas in 1924).

Art Groce's Springdale Store c1920's

Purchased from Raleigh True in 1923, Art Groce owned and operated this store across from the grade school for many years. When it burned in September 1963, many antiques dating from its earliest days were lost. Photo courtesy of Bob Groce.

In earlier days, two stores and a service station were located on the opposite corner. The first, built by Jonathan Richardson, was sold to John B. True, who added a creamery. When Mr. True passed away in March, 1915, his son, Raleigh True, became the store owner. Later in 1915, True attempted to build an addition to the store, which would have created a traffic hazard at that corner. A confrontation between Raleigh True and County officers developed when the County tried to remove the addition. The County offered Mr. True $750.00 to abandon his plans and remove the structure. In 1923, Raleigh True sold the store to Art Groce. Clyde Groce (Art's brother) added a service station just around the corner and Ernie Groce (father of both) built another store just south of the service station.

From Springdale, the highway (right at the flashing light) continues its graded ascent to Corbett. Approaching Corbett from the west, continue past the Corbett Christian Church (m 7.7 1), located at the intersection of the highway with Mershon Road. On this stretch, during the early '20s, Knighton's Confectionary and Grocery with a "barber shop in connection," stood almost directly across the highway from the present location of the church. Here, the highway again picks up the route of the

Columbian High School   c1924

This photo of Columbian High School was taken about a year after it opened its doors. The building has been in use for more than three-quarters of a century.

Photo courtesy of Ann (Reeves) Steers.

Corbett in 1959   Corbett Hardware, Scenic Area

Corbett Hardware store (1st building on left) as it appeared during the Corbett Centennial parade in 1959 and as it appears today (right).

1959 photo courtesy of Alice Wand. 2000 photo, the author.

former 'wire trail.' Beyond the church on the right, Schwartz's farm stand (m 8.0 r) sells fresh fruit in season, and the family's jams and jellies. Formerly part of the Taylor (a.k.a. Corbett) Estate, this property was purchased in 1920 by Louis 'Bill' Mershon, who had a home (since remodeled) built on the property before selling it early in 1921 to Frank Riggs. Riggs grew and hybridized flowers, and also had a flower stand, but it was located near the house. Entering Corbett, Cascade Utilities (m 8.3 l) appears. Across the highway, Owen Emily once operated a large flower stand, which featured daffodils, gladiolas and other flowers in season. The new Corbett Grade School now occupies part of the former Roy Emily place, of which there is no trace. The combined middle and high school complex is found just past the new grade school (m 8.5 r). Corbett High School (formerly Columbian High School), built in 1922-23, opened in September 1923, and has served the community since. When built, the high school building was painted white. In June, 1924, the Roy Emily family occupied the home adjacent (west of) to the former garage across

Arneson's Store

Arneson's store as it appeared in the mid to late 20's.

Arneson's Store, Scenic Area   c2000

Arneson's store as it appears today. Despite the provisions of the Scenic Area Act relating to the preservation of historic buildings, not much has been accomplished in this regard.   *Photo, the author.*

from the high school. That year, Emily purchased the former Corbett (a.k.a. Taylor) Grade School, and moved it to this location. Owen Allgood's garage, built shortly after WW II, is now an apartment building. The two vacant boarded-up store fronts to the east have become eyesores since the businesses closed some years ago. The first was formerly Corbett Hardware, built in 1924-25, and operated for many years by Claude Woodle. The second, the former Corbett Grocery, was built by Clarence Bush and Roy Anderson in 1923. In 1926, Louis H. Arneson purchased the store and operated it for approximately 18 years. Arneson's store had a lunch counter, and he did a brisk business preparing quick meals and sandwiches for travelers. When George and Vi Mershon re-

Corbett Christian Church c1914   Rickert's Garage c2000

The former church (left), completed in 1914, served the community for years. Clara (Lasley) Salzman recalls seeing an insulator imbedded in the maple tree in front of the church, a relic from the wire trail. The former Rickert's Garage (right) has been remodeled into apartments.   *Photos, the author.*

Corbett Grade School c1936

Corbett Grade School students return to school from summer vacation in 1936. Closed upon the completion of the new Corbett Grade School just west of CHS, the building was gutted by fire on October 6, 2001.   *Photo, the author.*

modeled Corbett Hardware after hardware sales declined, they put in a lunch counter, which also did very well.

Next on the right, past a residence adjacent to the high school, the former Corbett Cafe (m 8.6 r) is now a residence. After the cafe closed, Corbett School District utilized the building as its district office for about 20 years. The former Rickert's Garage, which was adjacent to the cafe on the east, has been converted to apartments. In 1919, Harry Rickert took over the management of the garage for W.R. Knight. Later, he purchased the business, which then became known as Rickert's Garage. In November, 1919, Jim Pounder purchased 17 acres south of the highway from the Corbett Estate. In the '20s, his son, Albert Pounder, developed the property. His business, Pounder's Truck Service, was located directly east of the garage. Pounder Oil Service continues to use the oil storage

Corbett (a.k.a. Taylor) Grade School c1921

This picture of the former Corbett Grade School was taken in 1921, part of a larger photograph that included Columbian High School to the east. When replaced by the new grade school completed in 1924, Roy Emily purchased this building for forty dollars and moved it to his property across from Columbian High School. Note the large maple tree that grew in the front yard of the Corbett Christian Church, which is partially visible behind the school.   *Photo courtesy of Larkin 'Buzzy' Shoultz.*

tanks at this location. The former Pounder home is situated adjacent to the former garage.

Almost directly across the highway is a building that housed Sig Knighton's store and barber shop (after he moved the business from the location mentioned earlier). In February, 1926, Knighton sold this store to Louis Arneson. (The author believes this building may have been built in 1914 by Clarence Deverell, who, the *Gresham Outlook* reported [June 12, 1914], "has established a confectionary store at Corbett." Subsequently, the building became 'home' to the Corbett Post, American Legion. Albert Pounder donated property for the Corbett Post Office, which is located a little east of his former home. Across the highway, the former Corbett Christian Church, built in 1913-14 and dedicated by Pastor Reeder on March 8, 1914, now houses a business, Servpro. The next large building (m 8.7 l) is the vacant, fire-gutted Corbett Grade School building, built on the site (and part of the foundation) of the first Columbian High School, which was destroyed by fire 79-years earlier (July 3, 1922). Knight's Grocery, just east of the former high school, also burned that day. Embers from the burning store set the school ablaze. The former grade school was first occupied by students in 1924-25. Two side wings were added in 1931, and the final, rear addition, in 1934. Corbett School District had planned to sell the historic building, which was gutted by a

Royal Chinook Inn

The Inn, a historical landmark owned and operated by the Reed family for several generations, recently re-opened as 'Corbett Station' under new owners. However, legal and regulatory problems caused its demise.   1953 photo courtesy of Steve Lehl.

fire on October 6, 2001. Across the highway from the grade school, Joe C. Van Zandt built a blacksmith shop to serve travelers as well a local farmers. Lewis Faught purchased the shop in the early '20s, and operated it until it burned in 1925.

The home just beyond the school (left) replaced Knight's store after the latter burned in 1922. Knight located his new store on this corner in 1915, moving from his previous store in Corbett "to the top of the hill" (*Gresham Outlook*, June 29, 1915). Walter H. Sinclair, who worked for Walt Knight and Knight's mother at the dance hall in 1919, recalled, "(I rustled) "wood for the La France Restaurant and dance hall. On Saturday nights I was the check room boy for the dance hall...Christmas that year, Walt Knight presented me with a suit of clothes. A couple of months later he got mad at me and charged me for it." The home now situated on the site was completed for the Harding family in 1925. It has been re-modeled several times and has undergone several changes in ownership since. At one time, John Flanagan operated a notions store in the building. Next (left) the Corbett Hill Road descends to the Columbia River, Corbett Landing and I-84. At its base, the former Royal Chinook Inn, since renamed Corbett Station, sits closed and vacant, another historic building and business facing an uncertain future. The former Reed home,

Settlemier (Chamberlain) Store and 'East' Corbett

The Settlemier Store, Chamberlain home (next right) and auto court (adjacent to the home) and the Bell Garage (that fronted the auto court) can be seen in this picture.
Photo courtesy of Pat (Bramhall) Paget.

Corbett Country Market c2001

The re-modeled store, now owned by Bill and Susan Leigh, has served the community since it was built by George Chamberlain in 1917. *Photo, the author.*

on the hillside just east of the Inn, was built in 1924 for Mrs. M.E. Reed by her sons to replace the home that burned in March, 1922.

Continuing on the main highway, the next business found is the Corbett Country Market (m 9.0 l). This store and gas station, built by George Chamberlain in 1917, is one of the few businesses to survive from its historic beginnings to the present. Between 1917 and 1922, Harley Bates became a partner in the mercantile business with George Chamberlain. In 1923, the store was sold to Perry Settlemier. Settlemier operated the store until 1958, when it was sold to Aaron Quinn. It is now

29

The Post Studio and an Advertising Handout

The interior of the Post Studio (left) at Chanticleer Point. The document on the right is a small handout describing the artist's work. Photos courtesy of Wes Post.

owned and operated by Bill and Susan Leigh. Adjacent (east), is the Chamberlain home, completed in October, 1917, which Nancy Wilson, Chamberlain's grandaughter, operates as a bed and breakfast. In the "golden" years, when the highway was the principal arterial east and west, the Chamberlains had an auto court, cabins, a campground and a flower stand on this eleven-acre site. In August, 1919, Chamberlain sold a parcel fronting the highway to Frank Bell. By November, 1919, Bell had completed construction of a garage and service station on the property. Also in August, 1919, Harley Bates purchased the next lot (adjacent to Bell's property) from Chamberlain. By the end of 1919, Bates had built a home on the property, and he moved into it with his family in January, 1920. In 1921, Frank Bell built a home adjacent to the garage. Both of these homes appear to be abandoned. The former Bell Garage no longer exists.

The Corbett Fire Hall is across the highway and next to it, the Crown Point RV Park. Around the bend, a log structure, Wayfarer Inn, built by Mrs. F.G. Cowing in 1925, served excellent meals. It burned as did a replacement structure (the latter in the late '50s). A residence sits approximately where the Inn was formerly located. A side road, Grange Hall Road, leads to the historic Columbian Grange building. The grange, established in 1893, first met in a rented building at lower Corbett. In 1898, this building became its permanent home. Continuing up the hill on the main highway, the former Julius Meier Estate, Menucha (m 9.9 l),

The View of the Gorge From Chanticleer

The spectacular view of the Columbia River Gorge from the Portland Women's Forum State Scenic Overlook (Chanticleer Point).   *Photo courtesy of Wes Post.*

comes in view. Meier purchased the property in April, 1914, and started construction on the estate in November that year.

Beyond Menucha is the Portland Women's Forum State Scenic Overlook (m 10.3 l), which offers an unmatched view of the Columbia River Gorge to the east. When the highway was under construction, artist Charles Wesley Post, painter, sculptor and etcher, established a small studio at this location. Post, born in Ohio in 1858, studied the grand masters in Europe for four years, 1874-1878. After his return, he taught art classes in the Twin Cities area of Minnesota. His first published work, *Twin City Etchings*, reflecting the interest of the artist in that medium, was well received. In 1907, Post moved to Portland. He found a parcel of land above Springdale, where he built a home for his family. Thus by 1912, he had located in East Multnomah County, and thereafter brought his artistic talent and skill to bear in rendering works reflecting the scenes his eye beheld, most particularly scenes in the Columbia River Gorge. He roamed the countryside in a horse and buggy with his faithful collie, Galla, at his side, and a couple of goats in tow. In addition to his artistic endeavors, Post carried a camera and recorded many of the activities he witnessed. Fortunately, he had established his studio at Chanticleer during the period when the highway was being built, and his photos add much to the historic record of those years. The author has been fortunate,

Chanticleer Inn

The Chanticleer Inn, overlooking the Columbia River Gorge above Rooster Rock Land-
ing, opened in 1912. Built for Alba R. and Madge Morgan, the restaurant thrived for
eighteen years. It burned to the ground October 8, 1930.
Photo courtesy of Ron Evans.

indeed, to have the family's permission to use these photos as well as other materials in their possession.

Close by Post's studio, the Chanticleer Inn, owned by Alba R. Morgan and his wife, Madge Kay, opened in 1912. Initially (or soon after the Inn opened), Margaret E. Henderson managed the restaurant and served as its hostess. On September 8, 1913, a second son, Richard, was born to the Morgans. Unfortunately, shortly thereafter Mrs Morgan died. Perhaps Mrs. Morgan's pregnancy caused Mrs. Henderson to be hired. On August 27, 1913, the Inn served as a meeting place for the Multnomah County Commission under Rufus Holman. At this meeting, Holman met with Sam Hill and the other backers of the highway. The next day, Multnomah County secured the services of Samuel Lancaster as engineer for the construction of the Columbia River Highway.

The Chanticleer became a well-known restaurant, attracting crowds of patrons from Portland as well as tourists after the highway opened. On Sunday, May 17, 1914, the Chanticleer Inn celebrated an "opening day," after extensive renovation of the facility by Mr. Morgan. Meanwhile, Mrs. Henderson became the manager of the Falls Chalet at Latourell, which opened a few weeks later. In February, 1916, Mr. Morgan brought a new bride, Marie Morgan, to Chanticleer. The Morgans owned and managed Chanticleer until it was destroyed by fire on October 8, 1930. Many individuals worked at Chanticleer during its heyday. Clara Mannthey maintained that President Woodrow Wilson "enjoyed eating

Young Ladies Who Worked at Chanticleer

Clara Mannthey   Crystal Pounder   Bea Faught

Clara Mannthey (left), reported that President Woodrow Wilson "enjoyed the biscuits I made." Crystal Pounder (center) worked banquets for the Morgans. Bea Faught (right) earned a dollar a day plus her room and board.
Photos courtesy of: left, Frieda O'Neil; center, Crystal Bayley; right, Sandy Cartisser.

Florence Wilson   Frances Knieriem   Elizabeth Morgan

Florence Wilson (left) caught a ride from Chanticleer Inn to Portland with the 'sodapop' man, with plans to elope with her sailor boy friend. Frances Knieriem (center) obtained her first 'off-the-farm' job at Chanticleer. Elizabeth Morgan (right) enjoyed working for the Morgans, though Marie Morgan "was awfully strait-laced."
1st and 2nd photos, '23 Cohimore, CHS; 3rd photo courtesy of Elizabeth Tanner.

Summit Station c1914

Summit Station, given the name because it sat at the highest point on the Columbia River Highway, was built by Frank Knieriem and Earnest Graff. The barn across the highway belonged to Jim Ross.   *Photo courtesy of Herb Salzman.*

the biscuits I made." During her teenage years, Bea Faught worked and boarded at the Inn. She earned $1.00 per day plus her room and board. Laura Hicks walked across the road to work at the Inn. Pearl Chamberlain worked at the Inn and at the Crown Point Chalet. The Morgans often called Crystal Pounder whenever they needed extra help for a large banquet. Edith (Miller) Butler and her sister, Myra (Miller) Wilson worked at the Inn, as did Myra's daughter, Florence. In 1923, Florence caught a ride from Chanticleer into Portland with the 'soda-pop man," where she expected to meet her boyfriend and elope. However, word reached her parents, who intercepted the 17 year-old prospective bride and thwarted her plans. However, her parents soon relented, and on July 7, 1923, Florence married Joe Eber, a sailor she had met in 1922 when Navy ships visited Portland for the Rose Festival. (In 1998, the couple celebrated their 75th wedding anniversary.)

At Chanticleer, the highway and the former 'wire trail' part; the latter descends to the former landing at Rooster Rock. Directly across the highway, the remodeled former Hicks family home stands. Just beyond (south of the highway), George and Carrie Gill built a store that did not survive the '20s. In 1919, W.G. Metzger, appointed Corbett Postmaster, moved the post office from (Lower) Corbett to his "place of business near Chanticleer Inn" (*Gresham Outlook*, March 21, 1919). In May, 1914, just past Knieriem Road, a small diner (m 10.6 l) that came to be known as 'The Summit,' opened as an ice cream parlor. Managed by Laura Ross,

The View Point Inn

The View Point Inn, designed by the renowned architect Carl Linde for the Grace H. Palmer Corporation in 1924, was owned and operated for years by William and Clara Moessner. In 1997, it reopened for a short time only to be shut down by Multnomah County. *Photo, the author.*

it was built by Frank Knieriem and Earnest A. Graff. Miss Ross, daughter of Jim and Mae Ross, served light lunches, coffee and ice cream. (Knieriem helped build several of the buildings in the vicinity, including the Chanticleer Inn, the Ross' barn and the Hanneman barn and home.) By May, 1915, Jim Ross had added a gasoline filling station, and announced that he would "also carry a few automobile tires and accessories" (*Gresham Outlook*, May 4, 1915). The "Summit" soon became another landmark on the highway. Subsequently, other owners managed the enterprise. Of these, Eva 'Ma' Hammer is most remembered. She purchased the business and operated it for many years as the 'Summit Tavern.' In the early '70s the building was demolished by the State Highway Department.

In 1921, almost directly across the highway, the Hanneman family had a large barn and home built. Mr. Hanneman ran a pure-bred Jersey herd and sold his dairy products directly to consumers at this location. He produced a soft ice cream for which he became locally famous. Eventually, it became a regular stop for tourists as well as local patrons. Earlier, when the highway came through, this area, formerly called 'Columbia Heights,' was the scene of a confrontation between a landowner and Multnomah County. Highway workers found "no trespassing" notices placed along the path of the right-of-way. A meeting ensued, attended by

Columbian High School Students Work at the View Point Inn
June Bates   Sophia and Augusta Lofstedt

June Bates, Sophia Lofstedt and Augusta 'Gussie' Lofstedt worked for Mr. Moessner at the View Point Inn. Gearhart Moessner, the owner's son, circled the tables and collected the waitresses tips (but not for them!).
    Left photo courtesy of June Kirby; Right photo courtesy of Gussie Kendrick.

Simon Benson, at which the owner was told that the County "could not afford to pay more." In response, "Benson put his hand on his pocket book and from there he took $100 and added to the sum that the court allowed and (the property owner) agreed to let them go." ("Columbia Heights," *Gresham Outlook*, September 20, 1914.) This incident illustrates the altruistic attitude demonstrated by business leaders of that era in overcoming obstacles to get the highway built.

Next, Larch Mountain Road intersects the highway. Drive up Larch Mountain Road about a quarter-mile to see the former View Point Inn. Designed by the renowned Portland architect, Carl Linde, the Lodge was built in 1924 by the Grace H. Palmer Corporation. In 1927, William Moessner, a chef trained in Germany, purchased the Lodge and renamed it the View Point Inn. This unique and beautiful inn, placed at a point with a stunning view of the Columbia River Gorge to the west, soon became a landmark in the area. Mr. Moessner and his wife, Clara, served gourmet meals to a distinguished clientele including political and business leaders, movie stars and others. Local girls who worked at the Inn include June Bates, June Butler, Gayle Hartshorn, Mildred Holtgrieve,

The Approach to Crown Point From the West

This stunning picture shows Crown Point after completion of the highway, but before the Vista House was built. Henderson's Chalet was located on the ridge above Crown Point. *Photo courtesy of Wes Post.*

Gussie Lofstedt, Sophia Lofstedt, Dorothy Martin and Phyllis Martin. Moessner had a son, Gearhart, who, the former waitresses report, would circle the tables and pick up the girls' tips. Dorothy Martin said that Mr. Moessner performed that duty when she worked there. The Inn became a regular stop for charter buses bringing visitors to the Gorge for a salmon dinner. Moessner closed the Inn in 1962, but continued to live on the premises until his death in 1979. The Inn is listed in the National Register of Historic Places. When an inventory of historic buildings was completed for purposes of the proposed Columbia River Gorge National Scenic Area, the Inn was closed, hence was not included as a commercial enterprise. Therefore, we have an incongruity - an Inn with a recognized historic importance that cannot now operate as an Inn. This is unfortunate, not only because of the historic significance of the building, but because it should be open for use by the public. [Its restrooms would be a welcome addition for visitors, particularly the elderly or disabled.]

Recently, after re-opening in 1997 under a very restrictive permit issued by Multnomah County, the new owners found themselves involved in a court case engendered by a complaint about its operation and parking. The Court found that the owners of the Inn had violated their operating permit. An appeal to the Gorge Commission failed for the reason cited above. Apparently, an Act of Congress would be required to allow the Inn to operate as an Inn. Hence, the View Point Inn joins the list of historic structures that have not fared well under the Scenic Area Act,

37

The Crown Point Chalet

The Chalet, owned and operated by Margaret E. Henderson, prospered from its opening in 1915 until it closed in 1930. In 1947, a subsequent owner, Mrs. Coffey, demolished the structure after it was vandalized.   Photo postcard courtesy of Steve Lehl.

despite its provisions related to historic preservation. After being open to the public for a short time, the View Point Inn is now closed.

From Larch Mountain Road, the highway begins a gradual descent to Latourell. Soon, Crown Point and the Vista House (m 11.4 r) come into view. Formerly, at the approach to the Vista House, W. Johnson opened an ice cream stand and confectionary (later, Johnson's Vista Cafe), which was situated on the right side of the highway. A small stand (later a gift shop) was located on the left. Johnson family members operated the cafe until it was sold to Mr. and Mrs. M.R. Moore. During the time the Johnson family owned the cafe, it was leased for a short period of time to Mrs. Gardner, who operated it as Gardner's Cafe. Doris Emily worked for the Johnsons and stated, "He was very pleasant to work for." She also related that her work day ended at eight o'clock, and her boyfriend, Lloyd Bramhall would pick her up. According to Doris, the couple then went to the Vista House parking lot to "watch the east bound 10:30 train go through the tunnel below." Bertha McKay also worked at the cafe, both for the Johnson family and Mrs. Gardner. In 1963, the structure was razed by the State of Oregon.

Another renowned restaurant, the Crown Point Chalet, owned and operated by Mrs. Margaret E. Henderson, was located on the ridge above the Vista House. This facility, with its famous decor, provided jobs for many Columbian High School students. The waitresses earned a dollar a day plus tips. They boarded at the Chalet six days per week, staying in dormitory rooms, with one day off to visit home. The workday com-

Crown Point Chalet - Interior Appointments

The extraordinary decor of the Chalet is remembered by the young ladies who worked for Mrs. Henderson. *Photo postcard courtesy of Elizabeth (Morgan) Tanner.*

Some of the Young Ladies Who Worked at the Chalet

From left, Mabel Harding, Dolores Morgan, Doris Emily and Inga Arneson. Mrs. Henderson treated her employes well, and often hosted CHS students at parties.
1st two photos, '23 Cohimore; 3rd, courtesy of Inga Myers.

Other Chalet Employees from Columbian High School

Grace Berney (top left), Arlie Kincaid (center) and Unknown (top right), 'ham it up' for Mrs. Henderson. Notice that one of the young ladies is wearing the Chalet's leopard rug shown in the picture on the preceding page. Mrs. M.E. Henderson (left), an elegant lady, taught her 'charges' well.

Photos (top) courtesy of Cliff Nelson.

Photo courtesy of Sandy Cartisser.

menced at 10:00 a.m. and concluded at midnight. The restaurant featured indoor and outdoor dining areas, a fine hardwood dance floor and Mrs. Henderson's renowned hospitality and chicken dinners. The unique dance floor, with its beautiful, smooth surface, was made of oak flooring laid edge to edge. Included among the many local high school girls working at the Chalet were: Inga Arneson, Grace Berney, Mabel Chamberlain, Mary Davis, Doris Emily, Anna Etling, Catherine Hall, Mabel Harding, Arlie Kincaid, Ruby McDonell, Nathalie Meter, Dolores Morgan, Agnes Soderstrom and Lucile Woodard. Inga related: "Mrs. Henderson trained us well and would brook no nonsense. Working there was fun, anyway." For several years Mrs. Henderson gave parties for CHS students, which Ted Berney remembers with fondness. "She was a generous person and the view from the Chalet was truly memorable." In 1928, Mrs. Henderson suffered a broken hip in a fall, and sold the Chalet

Excavating the Foundation for the Vista House c1916

This unique picture, taken by Charles W. Post, illustrates better than any text possibly could, the methods and means utilized to build the Multnomah County sections of the magnificent Columbia River Highway. Excavation for the foundation started in July, 1916.   *Photo courtesy of Wes Post.*

Construction of the Vista House c1917

This photograph demonstrates the construction method used to complete the exterior of the building. Local farmers, using teams and wagons, hauled most of the building materials for the structure from nearby mills or from Corbett. Erected as a memorial to Oregon's pioneers, the Vista House was dedicated May 5, 1918.

Photo courtesy of Zora Leona McCallum.

An Aerial View of Crown Point

This unusual view of the Vista House, taken in the '30s, includes the gift shop, Johnson's Vista Cafe and a service station to the south.   Western Ways postcard, the author.

soon thereafter. In 1947, the Chalet, vacant for some time and subject to vandalism, was demolished by a subsequent owner.

In 1910, the Multnomah County surveyor suggested that a road from the 'summit' to Latourell was not practical. Lancaster, assessing the situation at Crown Point, came up with a solution that involved building concrete piers along the cliff edge to support the highway. He placed concrete light posts every twenty feet along the protective railing on the outer edge of the viaduct that circles Crown Point, which, when lighted, does indeed provide Thor's Heights with a 'crown.' Sam Hill envisioned an "observatory from which the view both up and down the Columbia River could be viewed in silent communication with the infinite." Lancaster stated: "As a finale, it has been determined to erect at Crown Point where the roadway encircles the top of the great rock that stands sheer seven hundred and twenty five feet above the broad Columbia, a beautiful memorial building which will occupy the center of the circle and serve as an Isle of Safety to all the visitors who wish to look on that matchless scene. While this building is primarily a vista house arranged for the comfort of visitors, it is in reality a memorial building to the memory of the pioneers of Oregon, and this includes the living, as well as all of those brave spirits who have gone to their home on the other shore since they came into the Oregon country as pioneer home builders. The President and Governors of all the states will be asked to be present

42

The 'Figure Eight Loops'

A series of sweeping curves between the Vista House and Latourell keeps the gradient within Lancaster's limits.   *Photo postcard courtesy of Steve Lehl.*

when the great Columbia River Highway is formally dedicated early in June of 1916."

The Vista House, a reinforced concrete and stone-faced, octagonal structure designed by Portland architect Edgar M. Lazarus, is a fitting tribute to the pioneers it memorializes. Lazarus wrote: "The silent dignities of the pavillion with its outline against the sky will recall the ancient and mystic Thor's Crown (for) which the point was originally named." Now a State Park, the Vista House itself is managed by the non-profit 'Friends of Vista House' in cooperation with the Parks Department as an interpretive site and gift shop for visitors during the summer months. Lancaster credited Osman Royal for donating land in this area to Multnomah County. The East Multnomah Pioneer Association history credits Lorens M. Lund for donating the land upon which the Vista House was actually built (see "Historical Note," *Pioneer History*, 1982 Supplement, p. 80). In actuality, both donated land at Crown Point to Multnomah County.

The highway "impossible to build" continues east from the Vista House, descending in sweeping curves through the "Figure Eight Loops" (m 12.4-13.1) to Latourell Road (m 13.6 l). It is this stretch of the highway that likely engendered Lancaster's remarks about the "fern." At

43

The Latourell Footbridge c1916

The Latourell footbridge, built so that Guy Talbot could access his land across the highway, later provided a way for hikers to walk from Talbot Park to Latourell Falls.
Photo by Laura Mershon.

Latourell Falls Creek Bridge   ## Latourell Falls

Left: The bridge over Falls (Latourell) Creek looking west. The footbridge over the highway that formerly took one from Talbot State Park to Latourell Falls is visible in the background. A trail from the highway parking lot leads to Latourell Falls (right).
Left photo courtesy of Steve Lehl; right photo courtesy of Wes Post.

Maffet Home, Latourell Falls c1906

The Maffet home in Latourell was situated on the hillside along Falls Creek. Will Maffet used a 'Giant' (hydraulic mining device) to remove part of the hillside behind the home. Note Latourell Falls in the background.   Photo courtesy of Herb Salzman.

Latourell, the highway intersects the old wagon road to the "heights" or the "mountain," which in early days, was the route to and from Latourell for settlers living in the hinterland above. A dedicated County road, it is no longer maintained. It intersects Larch Mountain Road just beyond the 1-mile marker on that road. Before the Columbia River Highway connected the 'Summit' and Latourell, this old wagon road served that purpose.

The 'waterfalls' segment of the highway starts at Latourell, which Lancaster characterized in his book as "crystal waterfalls" formed by "little rivulets joined with mountain torrents, bringing the product of the glaciers down into the valleys..." Here Talbot State Park borders the town of Latourell lying below. Traces of the former Latourell Footbridge that crossed the highway are visible (m 13.6). Two local farmers, Frank Knieriem and Dave Butler, constructed this footbridge, which was part of the footpath from Talbot Park to Latourell Falls. The highway bridge across Latourell Creek and a trail to the falls are found at m 13.8 r. Before Mrs. Margaret E. Henderson opened the Crown Point Chalet, she hosted at the Falls Chalet, which formerly graced the hillside above this point on the eastern slope of Falls (Latourell) Creek. The establishment, owned by the Maffet family, burned in January, 1915, after being open

45

Maffet's Villa c1938

Maffet's Villa, built in 1916 by Harold Maffet, was razed by the Oregon State Parks Department in 1959. On September 2, 1945, Benjamin and Alice Bennett opened the restaurant as the Latourell Falls Villa and operated it until it was sold to the State.
Photo courtesy of Steve Lehl.

less than eight months. The owner, Harold Maffet, grew up in Brower, where his father owned a sawmill. By June, 1915, Maffet had rebuilt a "summer resort" named Falls Villa on the north side of the highway, which, the *Gresham Outlook* (June 15, 1915) reported, "Is now serving refreshments to tourists." In the '40s, it was purchased by Benjamin and Alice Bennett, who operated it under the name, 'Latourell Falls Villa,' until its closure in the late '50s. In 1959, the State of Oregon razed the structure and added the land to Talbot State Park. At one time, a service station was located where the parking lot is now situated. Later a gift shop replaced the service station.

Proceeding eastward from Latourell Falls, the next spectacular viewpoint is found at Shepperd's Dell (m 15.0), with its 100-foot arch spanning 150 feet. George Shepperd donated eleven acres at this point as a memorial park to his wife. Describing the tract as "unexcelled," Lancaster remarked: "Men of wealth and high position have done big things for the Columbia River Highway which will live in history; but George Shepperd, the man of small means, did his part full well." To see the "sparkling waterfall," described by Samuel Lancaster, proceed on foot down the path at the east end of the bridge. Just beyond Shepperd's Dell is the Bishop's Cap, part of which was removed in the construction of the highway to form a "half-tunnel" to improve overhead clearance. Beyond, the Luscher barn and home of the Fred Luscher family can be seen on the left (m 15.5 l). The Luscher family, Swiss immigrants, built the barn, a historic treasure, in the '80s. Luscher operated a dairy at this location and delivered milk to customers from Latourell eastward. During the construction of the highway, Fred had two teenage sons, Fritz and Ben,

Shepperd's Dell

The bridge at Shepperd's Dell with its 100-foot graceful arch spanning Shepperd's Dell Creek. The 'half-tunnel' at the base of Bishop's Rock can be seen in the in the background of the photo on the right.   Photos courtesy of Wes Post (l) and Steve Lehl (r).

each of whom drove a team pulling a Fresno scraper. Albert Salzman, who worked with the boys, recalled a conversation he had with Fred Luscher regarding the $5.00 per day each boy earned. Albert related that Fred, rolling his hands together, said, in his heavily accented voice, "Every two days a tventy."

Next (m 15.6 l) is Forest Hall (later known as the Maxwell House). Built for Nettie Arnold and Anne Hibler, it was considered one of the finer restaurants in the Gorge (a Springdale builder, George A. Canzler, helped with its construction). In 1938, Elsa Maxwell took over the establishment, and it soon became known as the Maxwell House. Bridal Veil State Park (m 15.9 l) includes Bridal Veil Falls among its attractions. Bridal Veil Lodge, across the highway, completed by Cecil Pounder in 1926, continues in business as a 'bed and breakfast' establishment. It is now owned and operated by Laurel Slater, whose great-grandparents, Virgil and Lillie Amend, purchased part of the property in 1895, some earlier. Another landmark in this locale is the former Sunset Gables, built by Milton F. Henderson. Henderson Road, just west of the Lodge provided access to his beautiful estate. In earlier days, a service station owned

47

Forest Hall

Forest Hall (a.k.a. Maxwell House), built for Nettie Arnold and Anne Hibler, became one of the more well-known structures in the Gorge. Later operated by Elsa Maxwell, it remained a popular restaurant for many years.   Photo courtesy of Steve Lehl.

Bridal Veil Lodge

The Bridal Veil Lodge, built for Virgil Amend by Cecil Pounder in 1926, is located across from Bridal Veil State Park. In addition to the Lodge, Amend built an auto camp with a number of small cabins for tourists. Virgil Amend's wife, Lillie, managed a restaurant in the Lodge. Laurel (Brown) Slater now operates the Lodge as a bed and breakfast.   Photo courtesy of Steve Lehl.

and operated by Iliff N. Long was located close by. Almost directly across the highway, the three-story, 18-room Cliff House stood, reportedly built

Mist Lodge (a.k.a.) Multnomah Lodge

Severely damaged by the heavy snowfall of 1921, Mist Lodge was rebuilt only to be destroyed by fire in 1929.   *Photo courtesy of Steve Lehl.*

in the late 1860s by George Ellesson's great-great grandfather. On October 9, 1947, a fire destroyed the structure.

(Note: Bridal Veil State Park has restrooms, which are sadly lacking [non-existent with respect to being handicap accessible] in the Gorge to this point.)

Continuing eastward, the former mill town of Bridal Veil soon appears (m 16.3-16.8). Of great import in the settlement of this area and the 'mountain' communities to the south, historic Bridal Veil is now owned by the Trust for Public Lands. There is some hope that the historic importance of Bridal Veil to East Multnomah County will be recorded on a monument to be erected at the site. To the east, the small town of Coopey Falls (m 17.2) [named after Charles Coopey]) is quickly passed. Once the site of a service station, tourist cabins and restaurant, only a few dwellings have survived, including those on the grounds of the beautiful convent of the Franciscan Sisters of the Eucharist.

Another of the many lodges that formerly served tourists along the highway, Mist Lodge (m 19.1 r) a.k.a. Multnomah Lodge, no longer exists. Located almost directly below Mist Falls, the Lodge roof collapsed from a heavy winter snowfall during the winter of 1920-21. Restored and reopened, it burned to the ground in 1929, and was not rebuilt. The

Wahkeena Falls   Multnomah Falls

Wahkeena Falls (left) descends in a series of cataracts, while Multnomah Falls (right), the highest waterfall in the Gorge, drops 620 feet in two spectacular cascades. In earlier days, sightseers reached this area by riverboat or by train.

Photos courtesy of Wes Post.

next landmark is Wahkeena Falls (m 19.2 r). Wahkeena consists of a series of cascades rather than plunging waterfalls. Prior to the flood of 1964, numerous attractive outdoor stone fireplaces built either by Italian stone masons or Civilian Conservation Corps (CCC) workers in the '30s were found here. The park was devastated by the flood, which turned each of the Gorge streams into raging, destructive torrents. In 1915, Simon Benson, Portland businessman and philanthropist, donated approximately 400 acres in this vicinity to the City of Portland. Thus both Wahkeena and Multnomah Falls came into public ownership. Later, the land was transferred to either the U.S. Forest Service or to the Oregon State Parks Department.

Finally, after traversing a viaduct (m 19.5) along a cliff face, Multnomah Falls (m 19.7 r) is reached. Multnomah is the highest (620 feet) and best known of the Gorge waterfalls. According to "Oregon Routes of Exploration," published by the Historic Preservation League of Oregon, Samuel Lancaster, while hiking the trail to reach the falls with Simon Benson, remarked, "Wouldn't it be nice if there was a footbridge across the lower water fall, with a path up to it? To which Benson re-

Benson Footbridge, Multnomah Falls

Multnomah Falls, with a close-up view of the new Benson Footbridge, donated by Simon Benson. *Photo courtesy of Wes Post.*

plied, "How much would it cost?" Lancaster calculated the cost on the spot, and Benson immediately wrote a check, saying, "Then go ahead and build it." Erected in 1914, the Benson Footbridge, named for its benefactor, replaced an earlier log bridge over the chasm. Multnomah Falls Lodge, constructed in 1925, continues to serve travelers on both I-84 and the old Columbia River Highway. The Lodge replaced an ice cream stand, Multnomah Hazelwood, operated by the Hazelwood Dairy, A premier tourist attraction for the State, Multnomah Falls attracts approximately 2.5 million visitors each year ("Oregon Routes of Exploration," above). In addition to viewing the falls, hiking one or more of the trails found here (or elsewhere in the Gorge) adds another dimension to the allure the area has for the visitor. Many of these trails were built or restored in the early '30s by CCC crews.

About two miles beyond Multnomah Falls, Oneonta Gorge (m 21.9 r) appears. The lower falls on the creek is accessible to the more adventurous traveler who is willing to chance walking up the creek about one-half mile. A trail west of Oneonta Gorge provides an opportunity to view the upper falls; however, be prepared for a long hike. The creek, flowing northward from the falls, follows an apparent fault to its mouth on the banks of the Columbia. At this point, the former military road, built through the Gorge in the 1870's, skirted the bluff immediately ahead. However, when the Oregon and Washington Railway and Navigation Company line was constructed in 1883, the old road was obliterated. In 1914, Lancaster solved the problem by tunneling through the obstacle. In 1948, the Oregon Highway Department filled the tunnel with rubble

Oneonta Gorge

Horsetail Falls

Oneonta Gorge (left) and Horsetail Falls (right) are among the many geological features enjoyed by visitors to the Gorge. Horsetail Falls is another of the Gorge waterfalls visible from I-84.
                                              Photos courtesy of Wes Post.

and re-routed the highway around the point. The highway passes so close to the next cascade, Horsetail Falls (m 22.2 r), that spray from the cataract sometimes douses the road. At one time, a restaurant, the 'Jack-O-Lantern,' operated by Mrs. W.J. Gebott, was found at this location. For a special hike, take the trail that leads above Horsetail Falls. This trail takes you to Ponytail Falls, which presents an unusual opportunity; you may walk behind a Gorge waterfall here.

Continuing east on the highway, the next landmark is Ainsworth State Park (m 22.7 - 23.3 r). Among its recreational opportunities are: hiking, camping and picnicking. The campground is found close to the intersection of the highway with I-84. Upon reaching that interchange, bear right and turn sharply to the right before entering I-84 in order to access the frontage road, actually the old highway. The former Hollywood Dairy (m 24.1 r), owned by Joe and Elma Bucher, served customers in the Gorge from Bridal Veil to Cascade Locks and across the river to Stevenson and environs, as well. In 1996, a devastating flash flood hit parts of Dodson, destroying the home of Hershel and Carol (Bucher) Royse, among other damage. Fortunately, the couple was able to evacuate their home minutes before the slide hit. The former home, which sits (2001) tilted among

The Bucher Dairy in Dodson

Joseph and Elma Bucher started their 'Hollywood Dairy' in 1930, with eight cows. They sold dairy and related products on both sides of the Columbia River. St. Peter's Dome is visible in the background. Photo courtesy of Carol Royse.

the rocks and flood debris, is a depressing sight. The town of Dodson, now haunted by the evidence of past glory, includes the former store building, which seems to be a repository for miscellaneous items that someone hopes to sell. A couple of derelict signs that formerly advertised motels stand abandoned, a gaunt reminder of the more prosperous days for roadside businesses before I-84 was built. When Bonneville Dam was under construction (1933-1938), Dodson became a temporary home for many families who worked on that project. Children of dam workers swelled school populations in the area, including the enrollment at Columbian High School in Corbett.

Continuing past Dodson, the former Sherman Inn (m 25.4 r) is now a residence. Alice Sherman, who decorated the Inn with a montage of furniture, relics, plants and souvenir plates, served her clientele for more than thiry years into the late '60s. The house specialty, Virginia baked ham, brought many return customers to the Inn. A '37 advertisement stated: "Shermans Inn, In summer COLUMBIA RIVER BAKED SALMON DINNER. All year 'round VIRGINIA BAKED HAM. Shell service and Products, YOUR SATISFACTION, OUR PLEASURE.

Beyond the former Inn, the branch road at the underpass (m 25.7 l) leads to the former location of the Warren Cannery and a pulp mill. During the years Bonneville Dam was under construction, Erick Enquist built a number of cottages here to house construction workers flocking to the area to obtain work. Continuing eastward, just beyond John B. Yeon State Park, (m 26.1) the old highway joins I-84 (from this point, the

The Moffett Creek Bridge

Lancaster characterized the Moffett Creek Bridge as the "largest flat arch bridge in America (1915) and the largest three-hinged arch in the world."

distances given will correspond to the mileage posts on I-84 - here, milepost 37.5). A hike up the Gorge trail here reveals a large pipeline that formerly took water to the pulp mill below to furnish the power needed to grind logs into pulp.

Between Warrendale and Cascade Locks, remnants of the old highway are found, including the Moffett Creek Bridge, but construction of the freeway (I-84) essentially obliterated much of the highway itself. Where found, remnants of the former highway have been restored and incorporated into segments of the Historic Columbia River Highway State Trail for bicycle and pedestrian use. There were homes and commercial structures along the former highway between Warrendale and Bonneville. When construction activity associated with Bonneville Dam started in 1933, Hal Babbitt and Rolf Enquist built a restaurant and bar west of Bonneville, the 'Bonny Villa' that attracted workers from the dam. Also in this area, the Columbia Vista Motor Lodge provided overnight accomodations for tourists. It sat above the railroad tracks on the north side of the old highway. The State Highway Department is now (2000) engaged in a project to reopen parts of the highway that were not totally destroyed during the construction of the freeway. In 1915, Lancaster described the Moffett Creek Bridge as "the largest flat arch bridge in America and the largest three-hinged arch in the world. The clear space is one hundred seventy feet and it rises only seventeen feet in that distance. The

Bonneville Station c1908

Bonneville Station, an Oregon Railway and Navigation Company station located at Bonneville, Oregon.   *Photo courtesy of Steve Lehl.*

Tyrell Tavern

The Tyrell Tavern, Bonneville, Oregon, stood on the south side of the old highway approximately where a parking lot has recently been built for visitors who wish to access remnants of the old highway between Moffett Creek and Cascade Locks.
                    Photo courtesy of Steve Lehl.

floor of the bridge is seventy feet above the stream." Access this segment of the Historic Columbia River Highway State Trail from the Bonneville exit.

The 'New' Tunnel at Bonneville

Completed in 1936, the tunnel re-routed traffic beneath the old highway, which had circled the point above the tunnel.
Photo courtesy of the Woodard family.

The exit at Bonneville provides access to several points of interest: the bridge (m 40.1 r) across Tanner Creek, segments, both east and west, of the former highway, Bonneville Dam, and the State Fish Hatchery on Tanner Creek. South of the freeway, park in the lot provided and walk portions of the old highway that lie between the Moffett Creek Bridge and Eagle Creek (or on to Cascade Locks). In the '20s, Sam Hill built a large home on top of the large rock formation north of I-84, east of exit 40. The house was razed in the late '50s. Approximately where the parking lot is now found, the Tyrell Tavern (m 41.2 r) once flourished, while across the road Lancaster established a campground and recreational facility, Camp Get-A-Way. A mercantile

The Eagle Creek Bridge

Because of Bonneville Dam, the water level is considerably higher now than when this picture was taken.
Photo postcard courtesy of Steve Lehl.

56

Penn's Tavern, Cascade Locks

Penn's Tavern, on the eastern outskirts of Cascade Locks, featured a restaurant, bar, dance hall and cabins.   *Photo postcard courtesy of Carol Royse.*

and a motel were found westerly of the tavern. The freeway exit at Eagle Creek leads to the native-stone clad bridge (m 41.5 r), one of the more famous structures on the highway and also one of the most photographed. To experience another segment of the old highway, walk from Eagle Creek to Cascade Locks. At the Cascade Locks exit (m 43.4 r), the same segment can be accessed by parking in the lot located just west of the Charburger Restaurant. Between Bonneville and Cascade Locks, the stonework laid by Italian stonemasons when the highway was built has been restored.

The old highway has been substantially obliterated by the construction of I-84 from Cascade Locks to Hood River. It is the main street through Cascade Locks after which it crosses beneath I-84 to continue east, paralleling the freeway. After crossing Herman Creek, return to the freeway at Herman Creek Road. Between Hood River and Mosier, access to much of the former highway is limited to hikers and bicycles. Recently, the twin Mosier tunnels were re-opened after being closed since the '50s. Restoration of significant remaining sections of the highway, as recommended by The Historic Columbia River Highway Advisory Committee, is an ongoing project. The section west of Mosier was completed in July, 2000.

Unfortunately, restoration of the Mitchell Point Tunnel is not possible. In 1966, the Oregon State Highway Department dynamited the

The Lindsey Inn, located hear Lindsey Creek between Cascade Locks and Hood River, was among a number of "roadhouses" that served travelers on the Columbia River Highway. *Photo courtesy of Steve Lehl.*

"Mitchell Point Tunnel of Many Vistas." Thus, in an instant, one of the most singular and unique features of the Columbia River Highway disappeared - reduced to rubble. Lancaster said: ... "The tunnel in the face of the cliff at Mitchell Point, with the concrete viaduct approaches, may well be considered among the most wonderful pieces of highway construction in the civilized world. It is fully equal to the famous Axenstrasse of Switzerland and one of the great features of the highway." Some contend the tunnel was destroyed because of safety concerns. However, similar geologic features, such as Bishop's Cap, which was undercut during the highway's construction, seems to be completely stable 80+ years later. The Swiss Axenstrasse is still extant; one cannot imagine its deliberate destruction by an agency of the State. In fact, in the '90s, the Swiss goverment undertook an expensive renovation project to save the tunnel. But the Mitchell Point Tunnel with its five 'windows' is gone. Built in 1915 and manifesting the vision and creative passion found in such luminaries as Sam Hill, Samuel Lancaster, Major H.L. Bowlby and John Elliott, its destruction by the State of Oregon is incomprehensible. In 1966, the Honorable Mark Hatfield served as Governor of Oregon; Glenn L. Jackson, Medford, served as Chairman of the Oregon Highway Commission. The location of the former Mitchell Point Tunnel is found near eastbound exit 58 on I-84.

The Mitchell Point Tunnel

The western portal to the tunnel at Mitchell Point. According to Lancaster, the tunnel at Mitchell Point surpassed Switzerland's Axenstrasse bordering Lake Lucerne, which served as the model for this marvel of engineering.   Photo courtesy of Wes Post.

A View of The Mitchell Point Tunnel from the Columbia River

This photo affords one an opportunity to view a stone cliff transformed into an artistic wonder, which was accomplished without detracting from the natural beauty of the area. The tunnel, carved through solid stone, was dynamited by the Oregon Department of Transportation in 1966.   Photo courtesy of Steve Lehl.

59

Mitchell Point Tunnel, East Approach

The east portal of the Mitchell Point Tunnel. Four of the five 'windows' that over-looked the Columbia River and provided a view of the Cascade Mountains in Wash-ington are visible.   *Photo courtesy of Steve Lehl.*

W.E. White's Mitchell Point Store

White's store, near the east portal of the Mitchell Point Tunnel, was another of the many business establishments that catered to travelers on the famous Columbia River Highway.   *Photo postcard courtesy of Steve Lehl.*

The Columbia Gorge Hotel

The classic Columbia Gorge Hotel is located on the Columbia River Highway at the west end of Hood River. Recently restored, it continues to serve visitors to the Gorge.
Photo courtesy of Steve Lehl.

Portions of the old highway can be found in Hood River. The highway runs parallel to I-84 as you approach exit 62, by which the Columbia Gorge Hotel north of the freeway can be reached. The hotel, designed by Morris H. Whitehouse for Simon Benson, opened June 21, 1921. Italian stone masons, who constructed the dry masonry walls, parapets and other stonework on the highway, built the stone walls and bridges at the site. During the '30s depression, the hotel was purchased by the Neighbors of Woodcraft as a retirement home. Restoration of the hotel, started in 1977, continues to this day. Now operated by the Columbia Gorge Hotel Company, the facility continues to attract tourists and others who have a taste for vintage elegance. The historic hotel is listed on the National Register of Historic Places.

At Mosier, automobiles can once again gain access to the highway, which leads to two exquisitely designed bridges, the Mosier Creek Bridge and the Dry Canyon Creek Bridge, both designed by Conde B. McCullough, Oregon State Highway Department Bridge Engineer. The highway continues eastward to the Rowena plateau and the Rowena Crest Viewpoint, which provides an unimpaired view of a quite different landscape from that experienced in the western sections of the road. Below, the highway descends to Rowena in a series of loops and turns that display Lancaster's maxim that the grade not exceed 5 per cent, and that turn radii be no less than 100 feet. The famous 'Mule Shoe' loop can be

Twin Tunnels, Columbia River Highway

The Twin Tunnels, west of Mosier, were filled with rubble and closed for many years. Recently, this portion of the highway was restored and opened for public access as part of the Historic Columbia River Highway State Trail. In this section, the highway is <u>not</u> open to automobiles.   *Photo courtesy of Steve Lehl.*

The Rowena Loops

The Rowena Loops take one from the Rowena Crest Viewpoint to the Columbia River below in descending, sweeping curves that illustrate Lancaster's grade and turn radius standards.   *Photo postcard courtesy of Steve Lehl.*

seen in a photograph above. After the descent to Rowena, the highway once again closes with its replacement and roughly parallels I-84 into The Dalles, the eastern terminus of the Historic Columbia River Highway.

The Columbia River Highway Descending to the River

This Markham photograph includes the Rowena Plateau from which the Columbia River Highway descends via the Rowena Loops to the riverbank below. The highway continued along the river into The Dalles. At an observance held near Rowena June 27, 1922, Simon Benson ceremoniously spread the last bit of paving material that completed the paving of the highway from Astoria to The Dalles.

Markham photo postcard, the author.

Frederick Villiers, Correspondent for the *Illustrated London News*, said on his tour of the Columbia River Highway shortly after its completion: "It possesses the best of all the great highways of the world... It is **The King of Roads**." In 1915, Lancaster said: "The way is now open, and as long as men and women continue to come and go through the Gorge of the Columbia they will see the mighty work of God and should glorify his name." To which the author would add: And see the incredible work designed and brought to fruition by an inspired engineer and all who participated in its construction, including many local farmers who lived along its path.

In 1921, Simon Benson, speaking of the highway and the scenic attractions opened to visitors because of its completion, said: "We have built good roads and invited the world to come view our beauty spots, but we have done nothing toward taking care of them after they arrive."

Benson's words are as appropriate today as when spoken. If visitors are to enjoy a leisurely tour of the highway and the scenic wonders to which it provides access, some amenities are necessary - an occasional restaurant, a place to stay overnight, businesses that cater to the needs and comfort of visitors and **restrooms** (which are currently scarce unless one knows exactly where to find them).

Touring the Columbia River Highway

Entrepeneurs soon had a thriving business taking tourists through the Gorge. This is Frank Shepard's Columbia Highway Bus, which he advertised as the "Only reliable bus, always running on time;" and "We employ courteous and careful drivers." His office was in the St. Charles Hotel, Portland. Photo courtesy of Steve Lehl.

Union Pacific Stage Line

Union Pacific Stages took visitors through the Gorge and provided Gorge residents with transportation to and from Portland. Advertising postcard courtesy of Vito Mosso.

Index

Sources and Notes

Lancaster, Samuel C., *The Columbia, America's Great Highway*, Self-Published, 1915.

Various, *History of the Columbia River Valley from The Dalles to the Sea*, Volume II, The S.J. Clarke Publishing Company, Chicago, 1928.

Most of the dates cited in the text came from *Gresham Outlook* articles written by "stringers" from Springdale, Corbett or Columbia Heights or from personal journals. Other sources are noted in the document.

Front cover print courtesy of Wes Post, grandson of Charles W. Post. On the back cover print (author's collection), the artist misspelled *Cascades*.